NATURAL RECORD BREAKERS

Jillian Powell

LEARNING
RESOURCES
EDUCATION
your schools library service

Heinemann Educational Publishers
Halley Court, Jordan Hill, Oxford OX2 8EJ
a division of Reed Educational & Professional Publishing Limited
www.heinemann.co.uk

Heinemann is a registered trademark of Reed Educational & Professional Publishing Ltd

First published 2000
Original edition © Jillian Powell 1998
Literacy World Satellites edition © Jillian Powell 2000
Additional writing for Satellites edition by Christine Butterworth

04 03 02 01 00
10 9 8 7 6 5 4 3 2 1

ISBN 0 435 11933 8   *LW Satellites: Natural Record Breakers* single copy

ISBN 0 435 11937 0   *LW Satellites: Natural Record Breakers* 6 copy pack

Photos: Ken Fisher / Tony Stone Images, page 5. Doug Scott / Chris Bonnington Library,
page 7. Georges Lopez / Still Pictures, page 8. Jorgen Schytte / Still Pictures, page 11.
Nick Haslam / Hutchinson Library, page 13. Kim Westerskov / Tony Stone Images, page
14. Tim Thompson / Tony Stone Images, page 17. Chris Sattlberger / Panos Pictures,
page 19. B. Regent / Hutchinson Library, page 21.

Illustrations: Steve Weston / Linden Artists, pages 4, 5, 7, 14, 20 and 22. The Maltings
Partnership, page 6. R.M. Lindsay, pages 9, 10 and 15. Julian Baker, pages 12 and 18.
Janos Marffy (Kathy Jakeman Illustration), page 16.

Thanks: Many thanks to Dr. Simon Carr of Oxford Brookes University for advising on the
manuscript, and to Helen Lantsbury of Oxford Brookes University for additional help.

Designed by M2
Printed and bound in the UK

Also available at Stage 2 of *Literacy World Satellites*

ISBN 0 435 11932 X   *LW Satellites: The Roman Chronicle* single copy
ISBN 0 435 11936 2   *LW Satellites: The Roman Chronicle* 6 copy pack

ISBN 0 435 11931 1   *LW Satellites: Have Your Say* single copy
ISBN 0 435 11935 4   *LW Satellites: Have Your Say* 6 copy pack

ISBN 0 435 11930 3   *LW Satellites: Life in Space* single copy
ISBN 0 435 11934 6   *LW Satellites: Life in Space* 6 copy pack

ISBN 0 435 11939 7   *LW Satellites: Teacher's Guide Stage 2*
ISBN 0 435 11938 9   *LW Satellites: Guided Reading Cards Stage 2*

Contents

Introduction

This book looks at natural record breakers, from the highest mountain to the deepest ocean.

It tells you where they are and how they were formed. It also tells you about some of the plants and animals that live near them.

The HIGHEST waterfall

A waterfall forms when a river flows over a rocky cliff.

Hard rock at the top will not wear away. But soft rock below will wear away. This can leave a step in the hard rock that the water falls over.

How a waterfall forms

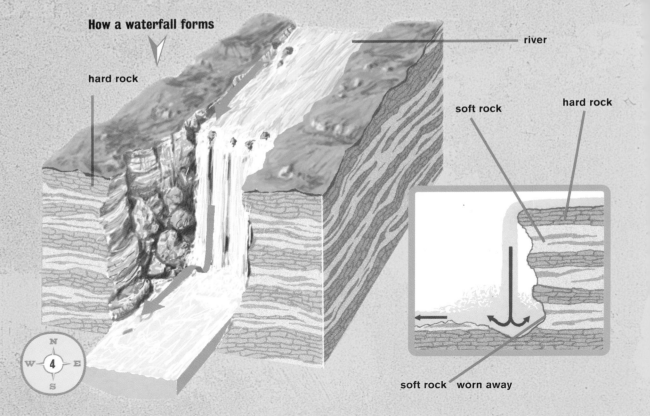

hard rock

river

soft rock

hard rock

soft rock worn away

Angel Falls

The highest waterfall in the world is in South America. It is 979 metres high, and it is called Angel Falls.

The waterfall is named after an American pilot called Jimmie Angel. In 1935, he was the first person to see it, when he was flying over mountains covered with jungle.

Angel Falls is as high as three Eiffel Towers standing on top of each other.

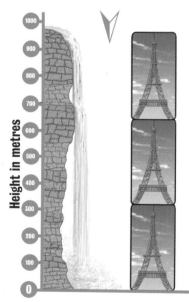

Height in metres

The Devil's Mount

The mountain at Angel
hidden in the mist. L
it the Devil's Moun

Above the falls,
Churun flows
edge of the
over the e

HIGHEST mountain

The surface of the Earth is made of huge areas called plates. They fit like a jigsaw. These plates are moving very slowly.

In some places the plates slowly push against each other. Where this happens, rock is pushed up to form fold mountains. This takes millions of years.

rocks are pushed up to make mountains

How fold mountains are made

two plates push against each other

Mount Everest

Mount Everest is the highest mountain in the world. It is in the Himalayas, and it is 8848 metres high.

The Himalayas are between two countries called Nepal and Tibet. The mountains are still growing as the plates push them up.

Mountain animals

Animals called ibex and yak live on the mountain. They are strong climbers and have thick coats to keep them warm.

Mountain people

The people who live in the Himalayas are called Sherpas. A Sherpa called Tenzing Norgay was one of the first men to climb Mount Everest. He climbed it in 1953 with Sir Edmund Hillary, who was from New Zealand.

The Sherpas tell stories about a monster called the yeti. They say it is over two metres tall and lives high in the mountains.

This chart shows the height of Everest and some other mountains.

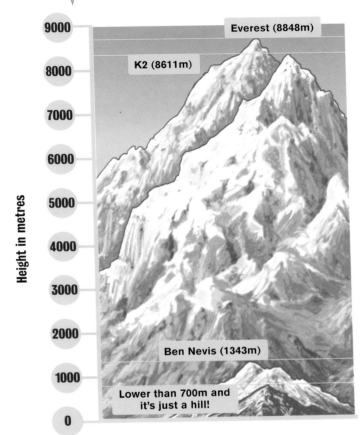

Height in metres

9000
8000
7000
6000
5000
4000
3000
2000
1000
0

Everest (8848m)

K2 (8611m)

Ben Nevis (1343m)

Lower than 700m and it's just a hill!

On high mountains the air is thin. Climbers need masks to help them breathe.

The BIGGEST desert

A desert is a dry place. Some deserts are cold and dry, like the Gobi Desert in China. The Sahara is a hot, dry desert in north Africa.

The Sahara Desert

The Sahara is the biggest desert in the world.

It is almost as big as the USA – 5000 kilometres from east to west, and 2000 kilometres from north to south.

Strong winds in the Sahara blow sand around the rocks. This erodes them. They are worn away into strange shapes.

The desert land

Some parts of the desert are flat, but other parts are steep and rocky.

Strong winds pile up the sand into tall dunes.

Desert plants

Plants in the desert can grow without a lot of rain. Cactus plants store water in their stems. Date palm trees have long roots that can reach water deep underground.

Desert animals

Living in the desert is hard. The days are burning hot, but the nights can be freezing cold.

Animals such as the fennec fox spend the hot day in underground burrows and come out to hunt only at night.

Camels can go for a long time without water. They live off the fat in their humps.

People who live in the desert are often nomads. Nomads travel from place to place to find food and water. The Tuareg people are nomads who live in the Sahara.

date palm tree

camels

Tuareg people

fennec fox

9

The LONGEST river

Rivers carry water off the land down to the sea. The force of a river can shape a valley, or give power to make electricity. Cities are often built on their banks.

The River Nile

The longest river in the world is the Nile in Africa. It flows for 6670 kilometres – as far as from London to New York!

The Nile is made from two smaller rivers, the White Nile and the Blue Nile. They join together and flow to the Mediterranean Sea.

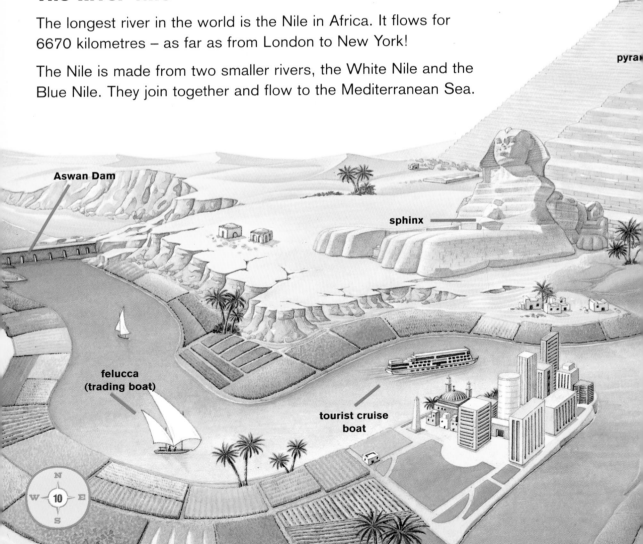

pyra▶

Aswan Dam

sphinx

felucca
(trading boat)

tourist cruise
boat

The city of Cairo takes its water from the Nile.

Nile floods

The Nile used to flood once every year. The Ancient Egyptians grew their crops in the rich mud left by the floods.

The Aswan Dam was built in the 1960s to stop the Nile flooding. The water behind the dam is called Lake Nasser. It is the biggest man-made lake in the world.

The lake provides water for farms, and for Egypt's cities. Cairo is on the banks of the Nile. It is Africa's biggest city.

Where does the Nile start?

The source of the Nile was found in 1875 by an explorer called Henry Morton Stanley. The river starts in central Africa at Ripon Falls, above Lake Victoria.

Nile animals and birds

Many animals, such as crocodiles and hippos, live in the Nile. Birds such as pink flamingoes and kingfishers feed on the fish in the river.

The BIGGEST cave

Caves are holes inside rocks. A cave is formed when rainwater drips into cracks in the rock. Over thousands of years, acid in the rainwater wears holes in the rock.

Most caves are formed in limestone rock

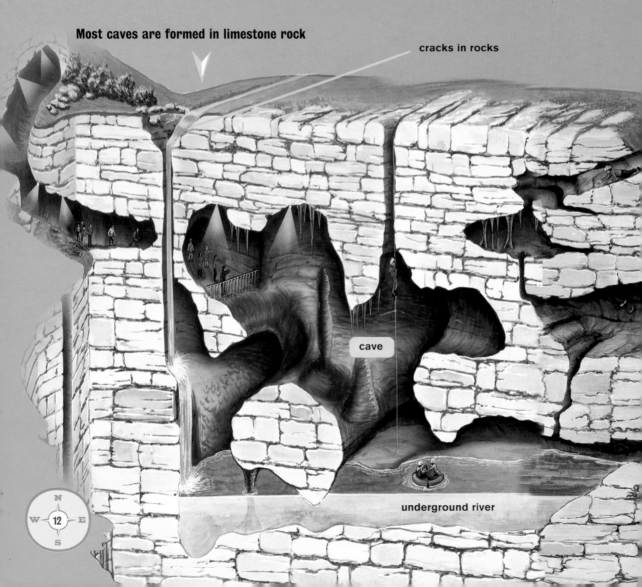

cracks in rocks

cave

underground river

N
W E
S
12

The Sarawak Chamber

The world's biggest cave is the Sarawak Chamber in Borneo. It was discovered in 1980.

The cave is 700 metres long – as big as 23 football pitches! The roof is up to 120 metres high.

 Inside the Sarawak Chamber

Inside the cave

Inside the cave it is very dark, damp and cold. Water drips from the roof onto the floor. The water has tiny amounts of chalk in it. This slowly forms rock pillars called **stalactites** and **stalagmites**.

Cave animals

The cave is home to many creatures. Birds nest in its walls. Thousands of bats hang upside-down on the cave walls. At night they fly out to hunt for food.

Spiders, snakes and scorpions live in the darkness of the cave floor.

The DEEPEST ocean

Oceans and seas cover more than two thirds of the surface of the Earth.

The Pacific Ocean

The Pacific is the biggest and deepest ocean on Earth. It holds half of all the seawater in the world.

Its widest part is from Malaysia to Central America. Here it reaches almost halfway round the planet.

The ocean floor

There is a huge valley at the bottom of the Pacific, called the Marianas Trench. The bottom of this trench is 11 kilometres below the surface.

This is the deepest place on Earth. If you dropped a kilogram weight into the water, it would take an hour to reach the bottom of the trench.

The Pacific has 25,000 islands – more than all the other oceans put together.

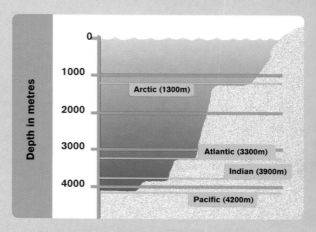

This chart shows the depth of all the oceans in the world

Ocean explorers

Two thousand years ago, sailors crossed the Pacific on rafts.
Today, explorers go down in special craft to find deep-sea creatures.

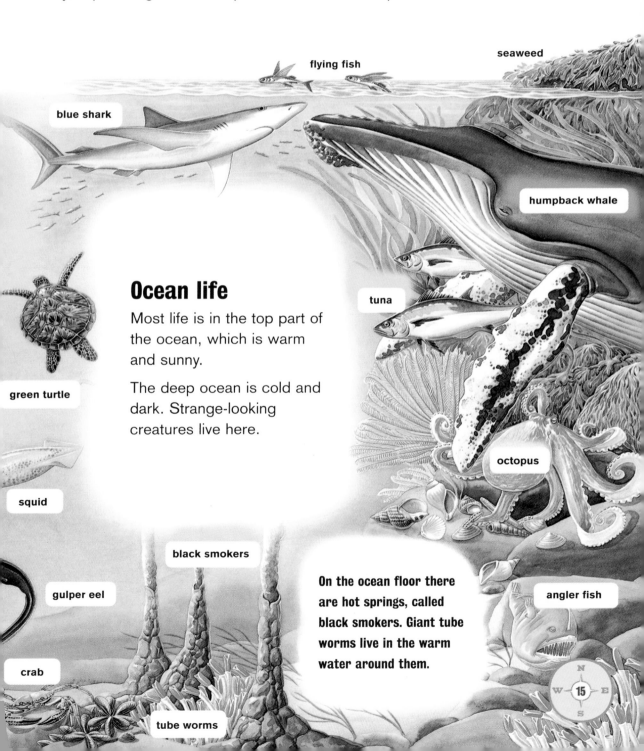

flying fish

seaweed

blue shark

humpback whale

Ocean life

Most life is in the top part of
the ocean, which is warm
and sunny.

The deep ocean is cold and
dark. Strange-looking
creatures live here.

tuna

green turtle

octopus

squid

black smokers

gulper eel

On the ocean floor there
are hot springs, called
black smokers. Giant tube
worms live in the warm
water around them.

angler fish

crab

tube worms

The LONGIEST glacier

A glacier is a river of ice. Glaciers form in the coldest parts of the world, where snow has fallen for thousands of years. As the snow piles up, the bottom layer turns to ice.

The ice layer gets so heavy that it starts to move. The huge glacier slowly pushes rocks along with it. This scrapes out a deep valley from the land below.

smaller glacier joining from the side

The end of a glacier is called the 'snout'. Here the ice begins to melt.

glacier snout

ier head

An iceberg is a chunk of ice that breaks off from the snout of the
glacier. You can see only a small part of an iceberg above the water.

The Lambert Glacier

The longest glacier in the
world is as long as 14
Channel Tunnels. It is the
Lambert Glacier in Antarctica,
near the South **Pole**.

It is 64 kilometres wide and
708 kilometres long.

Wildlife in Antarctica

Penguins and seals live in
Antarctica. Fish in these icy
waters have special blood to
stop them freezing.

The BIGGEST
live volcano

The centre of the Earth is full of fire and molten rock. A volcano **erupts** when the fire bursts from a hole in the Earth's **crust**.

Gas, ash and red-hot rock called **lava** erupt from the top of the volcano. There are about 850 live volcanoes in the world.

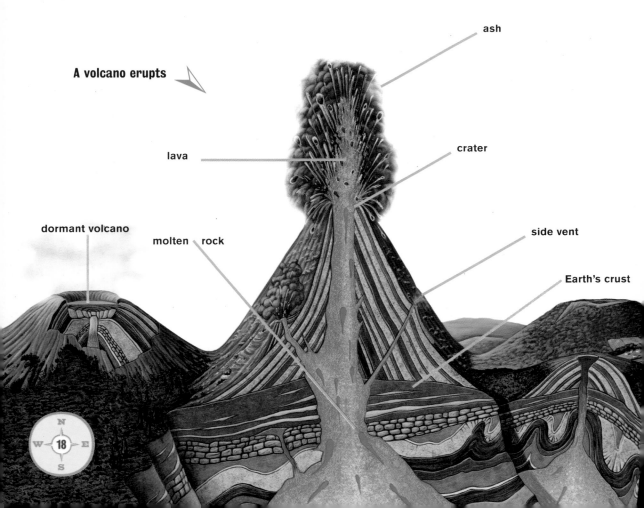

A volcano erupts

ash

lava

crater

dormant volcano

molten rock

side vent

Earth's crust

Mauna Loa

The biggest live volcano in the world is Mauna Loa, on the island of Hawaii. It is one of a ring of live volcanoes around the Pacific Ocean.

Mauna Loa, which means Long Mountain, is 9000 metres high. Most of it is under the sea.

Clouds of steam and gas rise from the volcano.

Around the volcano

Hot springs of water and hot mud pools bubble up. The gas from underground smells like bad eggs.

Volcanic rock

The red-hot river of lava flows down the volcano. Slowly it cools and hardens into a dark rock called basalt.

The BIGGEST gorge

A gorge is a deep valley between steep walls of rock.
It can be formed in one of two ways:
1. Some gorges are cut by river water slowly wearing
   down into the rock.
2. Other gorges are made when an underground river
   forms a cave, then the roof falls in.

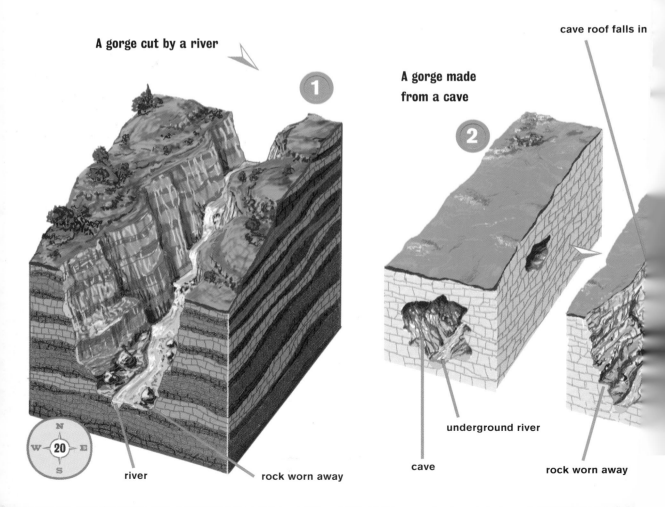

A gorge cut by a river

1

**A gorge made
from a cave**

2

cave roof falls in

underground river

cave

rock worn away

river

rock worn away

The Grand Canyon

The biggest gorge in the world is the Grand Canyon in Arizona, USA.

The Grand Canyon is 450 kilometres long and 60 million years old. It was cut in the time of the dinosaurs, by the Colorado River.

The gorge is 29 kilometres wide at the top, and 1.6 kilometres deep. It takes a whole day to walk down to the river and back up.

Two sorts of climate

The gorge is so deep that it has different **climates** at the top and bottom.

At the top it is often cold, and there can be deep snow in winter. At the bottom is hot, dry desert.

The Colorado River.

Plants and animals

Deer and squirrels live near the top of the gorge. Grey foxes and chipmunks live on the cool sides.

Cactus plants grow at the bottom. Here scorpions, snakes and lizards live.

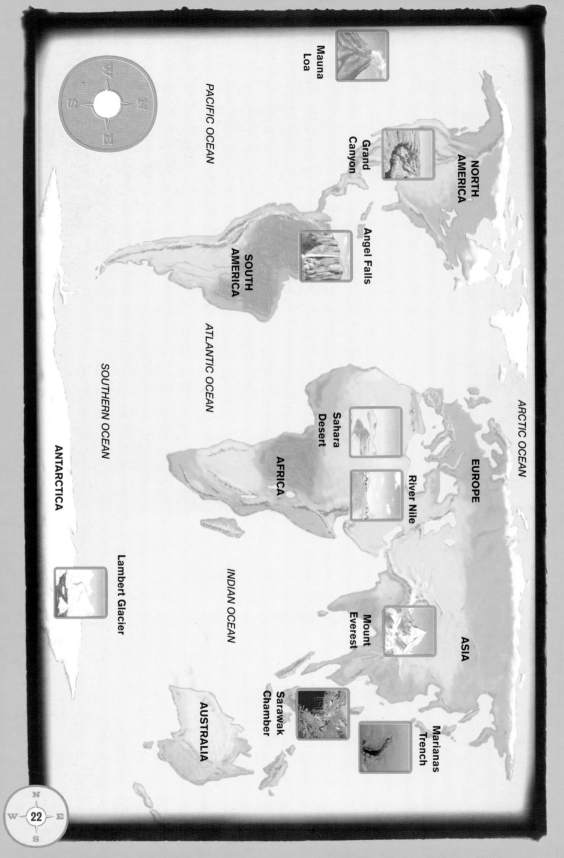

Mauna Loa

PACIFIC OCEAN

Grand Canyon

NORTH AMERICA

Angel Falls

SOUTH AMERICA

ATLANTIC OCEAN

ARCTIC OCEAN

Sahara Desert

AFRICA

River Nile

EUROPE

SOUTHERN OCEAN

ANTARCTICA

Lambert Glacier

INDIAN OCEAN

Mount Everest

ASIA

Sarawak Chamber

Marianas Trench

AUSTRALIA